1001

Amazing

Jokes

Jack Goldstein

Andrews UK Limited

First published worldwide in 2013 by
Andrews UK Limited
The Hat Factory
Bute Street
Luton, LU1 2EY
www.andrewsuk.com

A million thanks to Jimmy Russell
"Shh no tears, only dreams now."

Contents

The Jokes

Jokes for Everyone

General Jokes - Part 1

Why did the clown go to the doctor?
Because he was feeling a little funny!

What did the water say to the boat?
Nothing, it just waved!

How did the Vikings send secret messages?
By Norse code!

What is a robot's favorite type of music?
Heavy metal!

Where did the king keep his armies?
In his sleevies!

What kind of lighting did Noah use for the ark?
Floodlights!

Why can't a bicycle stand up by itself?
Because it's two-tired!

Why was the broom late?
It over swept!

Why do golfers wear two pairs of pants?
In case they get a hole in one!

Why did the scientist install a knocker on his door?
To win the Nobel prize!

Animals

Where do polar bears vote?
The North Poll!

Why do cows wear bells?
Because their horns don't work!

How do you talk to a fish?
You drop him a line!

What animal should you never play cards with?
A cheetah!

How do you catch a squirrel?
Climb up a tree and act like a nut!

What color socks do bears wear?
They don't wear socks, they have bear feet!

What's black and white, black and white, black and white?
A penguin rolling down a hill!

What did the fish say when he swam into the wall?
Dam!

How do bees get to school?
By school buzz!

Why do bees have sticky hair?
Because they use honeycombs!

Crossing the Road

Why did the chicken cross the road?
To get to the other side!

Why did the chicken cross the playground?
To get to the other slide!

Why did the rooster cross the road?
To cockadoodle dooo something!

Why did the turkey cross the road?
To prove he wasn't chicken!

Why did the dinosaur cross the road?
Because chickens hadn't been invented back then!

Why did the horse cross the road?
Because the chicken needed a day off!

Why did the cow cross the road?
To get to the udder side!

Why did the chicken cross the road halfway?
She wanted to lay it on the line!

Why didn't the skeleton cross the road?
Because he didn't have the guts!

Why did the clairvoyant cross the road?
To get to 'the other side'!

In the Bar

A Horse walks into a bar...
The bartender says, "So. Why the long face?"

A man walks into a bar and asks the bartender, "Do you have any helicopter flavored crisps?"
The bartender shakes his head and says, "No, we only have plain."

A potato walks into a bar...
all eyes were on him!

A man walks into a bar with a lump of tarmac under his arm. 'What would you like?' asks the barman.
The man replies, 'A pint of beer and one for the road.'

A skeleton walks into a bar...
He says, 'I'd like a beer and a mop!'

Thomas Edison walks into a bar...
The bartender says, "I'll serve you a beer, just don't get any ideas."

The barman says, "We don't serve time travellers in here."
A time traveller walks into a bar...

A priest, a rabbi, and a vicar walk into a pub.
The barman says, 'Is this some kind of joke?'

A bear walks into a bar and says 'I'll have a whisky and... soda.' The bartender says, 'Why the big pause?'
'Dunno,' says the bear. 'I've always had them!'

A hippopotamus walks into a bar and asks the barman for a pint. "That will be ten dollars please" says the barman. The hippo pays and starts to sip his beer. "You know we don't get many hippos in here" says the barman.
The hippo replies: "At ten dollars a drink I'm not surprised!".

Criss Cross

What do you get when you cross a cow with a trampoline?
A milkshake!

What do you get when you cross a caterpillar and a parrot?
A walkie talkie!

What do you get when you cross a fish with an elephant?
Swimming trunks!

What do you get when you cross a karate expert with a pig?
A pork chop!

What do you get when you cross a lemon and a
cat?
A sourpuss!

What do you get if you cross a kangaroo and an
elephant?
Big holes all over Australia!

What do you get when you cross Batman & Robin
with a steamroller?
Flatman & Ribbon!

What do you get when you cross a wolf and an egg?
A very hairy omelette!

What do you get when you cross a galaxy with a
toad?
Star Warts!

What do you get when you cross a python with a
porcupine?
Ten feet of barbed wire!

The Sea

How do sailors wash their clothes?
*They throw their laundry overboard and it's washed
ashore!*

What's a pirate's favourite country?
Aaaaaaaaaaaargentina!

What has 8 legs and 8 eyes?
8 Pirates!

Why is it so easy to weigh fish?
They have their own scales!

What happens when you cross a great white shark with a cow?
I don't know but I wouldn't want to milk it!

What lies at the bottom of the sea and shakes?
A nervous wreck!

What did the mummy sardine tell her children when they saw a submarine?
Don't worry, it's only a tin of people!

Why do seagulls fly over the sea?
Because if they flew over the bay they would be bagels!

What's a pirate's favourite Star Wars character?
Arrrrrrrrr 2 D 2!

What did one rock pool say to the other rock pool?
Show me your mussels!

Science

What do you do with dead chemists?
Barium!

What's a nuclear physicist's favorite meal?
Fission chips!

What kind of ghosts haunt chemistry labs?
Methylated Spirits!

Who solves mysteries involving electricity?
Sherlock Ohms!

Where does bad light go?
To prism!

Schrodinger's cat walks into a bar...
And doesn't!

An ion walks into a bar, says "I've lost an electron".
The barman says "are you sure?"
The electron replies "yes, I'm positive!"

What did one electron say to the other electron?
Don't get excited. You'll only get into a state!

There was a sale on particles the other week...
Neutrons were free of charge!

Do you know any jokes about sodium?
Na!

Rude Jokes

What flies through the air and stinks?
A smelly-copter!

What is invisible and smells like carrots?
Bunny Farts!

Why did the baker have smelly hands?
Because he kneaded a poo!

What's yellow and smells of bananas?
Monkey sick!

Why do mice have little balls?
Because they like to dance!

What's pink, wrinkled and hangs out your pyjamas?
Your mother!

Why did the beach blush?
Because the sea weed!

What's brown, sounds like a bell and comes out of a cow backwards?
DUNG!

Why did Tigger put his head in the toilet?
Because he was looking for Pooh!

Knock knock...
Who' there...
Smell mop...
Smell mop who?
Yuk! No way!

General Jokes - Part 2

Why was the robot angry?
Because someone kept pushing his buttons!

Why was 6 afraid of 7?
Because: 7 8 9!

What is brown and sticky?
a stick!

When is a car not a car?
When it turns into a garage!

Did you hear the joke about the roof?
Never mind, it's over your head!

There are two fish in a tank...
One says to the other, "So how do you drive this thing?"

What was 30 feet long, had a two-foot-long beak, and left crumbs all over the mattress?
Pretzelcoatlus!

Why are chefs cruel?
Because they batter fish, beat eggs and whip cream!

Why did the clock in the cafeteria always run slow?
Every lunch it went back four seconds!

If you hear of any jokes about fish, will you let minnow?

The Best Jokes

What's green and smells like blue paint?
Green paint!

How do you make a bandstand?
Take away their chairs!

What is green and stands in the corner?
A naughty frog!

Why does it take pirates so long to learn the alphabet?
Because they spend years at C!

What has four wheels and flies?
A garbage truck!

What lies in a pram and wobbles?
A jelly baby!

What's did one tomato say to the other tomato?
You go ahead and I'll ketchup!

What's the difference between a guitar and a fish?
You can't tuna fish!

What did one snowman say to the other?
"Can you smell carrots?"

What does a nosey pepper do?
Gets jalapeño business!

Knock Knock Jokes

General Jokes – Part 1

Knock, knock.
Who's there?
Canoe.
Canoe who?
Canoe help me with my homework?

Knock, knock.
Who's there?
Luke.
Luke who?
Luke through the keyhole and you'll see!

Knock, knock.
Who's there?
Scott.
Scott who?
Scott nothing to do with you.

Knock, knock.
Who's there?
Sam.
Sam who?
Sam person who knocked on the door last time!

Knock, knock.
Who's there?
Aaron.
Aaron who?
Aaron the side of caution!

Knock, knock.!
Who's there?
To.
To who?
To whom, actually.

Knock, knock.
Who's there?
Odysseus.
Odysseus who?
Odysseus just the last straw!

Knock, knock.
Who's there?
Tennis.
Tennis who?
Tennis Five plus Five!

Knock, knock.
Who's there?
Sacha.
Sacha who?
Sacha fuss, just because I knocked on your door!

Knock, knock.
Who's there?
Genoa.
Genoa who?
Genoa any good knock knock jokes?

Who's Knocking - Part 1

Knock, knock.
Who's there?
Iva.
Iva who?
I've a sore hand from knocking!

Knock, knock.
Who's there?
Avenue.
Avenue who?
Avenue knocked on this door before?

Knock, knock.
Who's there?
Harry.
Harry who?
Harry up, it's cold out here!

Knock, knock.
Who's there?
Norma Lee.
Norma Lee who?
Norma Lee I don't go around knocking on doors!

Knock, knock.
Who's there?
Abbot.
Abbot who?
Abbot you don't know who this is!

Knock, knock.
Who's there?
A herd.
A herd who?
A herd you were home, so I came over!

Knock, knock.
Who's there?
Ben.
Ben who?
Ben knocking for ten minutes!

Knock, knock.
Who's there?
Lettuce.
Lettuce who?
Lettuce in, it's cold out here.

Knock, knock.
Who's there?
Freighter.
Freighter who?
Freighter open the door, are you?

Knock, knock.
Who's there?
Doris.
Doris who?
Doris locked, that's why I'm knocking!

Silly Jokes - Part 1

Knock, knock.
Who's there?
Arfur.
Arfur who?
Arfur got!

Knock, knock.
Who's there?
Tank.
Tank who?
Your welcome!

Knock, knock.
Who's there?
Nana.
Nana who?
Nana your business.

Knock, knock.
Who's there?
Annetta.
Annetta who?
Annetta wisecrack and you're out of here!

Knock, knock.
Who's there?
Boo.
Boo who?
Was my joke so bad it made you cry?

Knock, knock.
Who's there?
A little old lady.
A little old lady who?
That's some good yodelling there!

Knock, knock.
Who's there?
Ya.
Ya who?
Well you sound pleased to see me!

Knock, knock.
Who's there?
Justin.
Justin who?
Just in the neighbourhood, thought I would drop by.

Knock, knock.
Who's there?
Alex.
Alex who?
Alex-plain later!

Knock, knock.
Who's there?
Sadie.
Sadie who?
Sadie magic word and watch me disappear!

Animals

Knock, knock.
Who's there?
Cows go.
Cows go who?
Cows go moo, not who!

Knock, knock.
Who's there?
Gorilla.
Gorilla who?
Gorilla cheese sandwich for me and I'll be right over.

Knock, knock.
Who's there?
Althea.
Althea who?
Althea later alligator!

Knock, knock.
Who's there?
Jaws.
Jaws who?
Jaws truly!

Knock, knock.
Who's there?
Hoo.
Hoo who?
Are you an owl?

Knock, knock.
Who's there?
The impatient cow.
The impatient cow...
(interrupting) Mooooo!

Knock, knock.
Who's there?
Honey bee.
Honey bee who?
Honey bee a dear and OPEN THIS DOOR!

Knock, knock.
Who's there?
Iguana.
Iguana who?
Iguana hold your hand!

Knock, knock.
Who's there?
Rhino.
Rhino who?
Rhino every knock-knock joke there is!

Knock, knock.
Who's there?
Cuckoo Catch.
Cuckoo Catch Who?
(sing) Mrs. Robinson, Jesus loves you more than you will know...

General Jokes - Part 2

Knock, knock.
Who's there?
Hannah.
Hannah who?
Hannah partridge in a pear tree!

Knock, knock.
Who's there?
Yule.
Yule who?
Yule never know!

Knock, knock.
Who's there?
Merry.
Merry who?
Merry Christmas!

Knock, knock.
Who's there?
Franz.
Franz who?
Franz, Romans, Countrymen...

Knock, knock.
Who's there?
Winnie Thup.
Winnie Thup who?
Yes, and Tigger is here as well!

Knock, knock.
Who's there?
Maida.
Maida who?
Maida force be with you!

Knock, knock.
Who's there?
Mae.
Mae who?
Mae be I'll tell you or Mae be I won't...

Knock, knock.
Who's there?
Hal.
Hal who?
Hal who to you too!

Knock, knock.
Who's there?
Eve.
Eve who?
Eve who my hearties!

Knock, knock.
Who's there?
Venice.
Venice who?
Venice this door gonna open?

Who's Knocking - Part 2

Knock, knock.
Who's there?
Ivor.
Ivor who?
Ivor you let me in or I'll climb through the window.

Knock, knock.
Who's there?
Major.
Major who?
Major answer, didn't I!

Knock, knock.
Who's there?
Ken.
Ken who?
Ken I come in or do I have to climb through a window?

Knock, knock.
Who's there?
Alexia.
Alexia who?
Alexia again to open this door!

Knock, knock.
Who's there?
Ferdie.
Ferdie who?
Ferdie last time open this door!

Knock, knock.
Who's there?
Fozzie.
Fozzie who?
Fozzie hundredth time let me in!

Knock, knock.
Who's there?
Spain.
Spain who?
Spain to have to keep knocking on this door!

Knock, knock.
Who's there?
Snow.
Snow who?
Snow use, I've forgotten my key again!

Knock, knock.
Who's there?
Harmony.
Harmony who?
Harmony times are we going to go through this?

Knock, knock.
Who's there?
Waddle.
Waddle who ?
Waddle you give me if I go away?

Silly Jokes - Part 2

Knock, knock.
Who's there?
Daisy.
Daisy who?
(Sing) Daisy me rollin, dey hatin…

Knock, knock.
Who's there?
Kenya!
Kenya who?
Kenya guess who is it?

Knock, knock.
Who's there?
Juicy.
Juicy who?
Juicy what I just saw?

Knock, knock.
Who's there?
Etch.
Etch who?
Bless you!

Knock, knock.
Who's there?
Jerrold.
Jerrold who?
Jerrold friend, that's who!

Knock, knock.
Who's there?
Aladdin.
Aladdin who?
Aladdin the street wants a word with you!

Knock, knock.
Who's there?
Carrie
Carrie who?
Carrie me home, my feet are tired!

Knock, knock.
Who's there?
No-one.
No-one who?
(Remain silent!)

Knock, knock.
Who's there?
Jean.
Jean who?
Jeanius - you just don't recognise it!

Knock, knock.
Who's there?
Alex.
Alex who?
Alex the questions round here!

Food and Drink

Knock, knock.
Who's there?
Noah.
Noah who?
Noah good place we can get something to eat?

Knock, knock.
Who's there?
Doctor.
Doctor who?
No, Dr. Pepper!

Knock, knock.
Who's there?
Doughnut.
Doughnut who?
Doughnut worry, it's just a Knock, knock. joke!

Knock, knock.
Who's there?
Figs.
Figs who?
Figs the doorbell, it's broken!

Knock, knock.
Who's there?
Ice cream.
Ice cream who?
Ice cream if you don't let me in!

Knock, knock.
Who's there?
Cash.
Cash who?
No thanks, I'd prefer a peanut.

Knock, knock.
Who's there?
Ketchup.
Ketchup who?
Ketchup with me and I'll tell you!

Knock, knock.
Who's there?
Butter.
Butter who?
Butter open quick, I'm desperate for the bathroom!

Knock, knock.
Who's there?
Dimitri.
Dimitri who?
Dimitri is where di burgers grow!

Knock, knock.
Who's there?
Lettuce.
Lettuce who?
Lettuce try this again tomorrow.

Who's Knocking - Part 3

Knock, knock.
Who's there?
Jester.
Jester who?
Jester minute I'm trying to find my keys!

Knock, knock.
Who's there?
Howl.
Howl who?
Howl you know unless you open the door?

Knock, knock.
Who's there?
Dozen.
Dozen who?
Dozen anybody want to let me in?

Knock, knock.
Who's there?
Scold.
Scold who?
Scold enough out here to go ice skating.

Knock, knock.
Who's there?
Isadore.
Isadore who?
Isadore locked?, I can't get in!

Knock, knock.
Who's there?
Ahmed.
Ahmed who?
Ahmed a big mistake coming here!

Knock, knock.
Who's there?
Isabella.
Isabella who?
Isabella out of order?

Knock, knock.
Who's there?
Adore.
Adore who?
Adore is between us. Open up!

Knock, knock.
Who's there?
Police.
Police who?
Police hurry up, it's chilly outside!

Knock, knock.
Who's there?
Jewell.
Jewell who?
Jewell know if you open the door!

General Jokes - Part 3

Knock, knock.
Who's there?
Thermos.
Thermos who?
Thermos be a better knock-knock joke than this!

Knock, knock.
Who's there?
Evan.
Evan who?
Evan you should know who it is.

Knock, knock.
Who's there?
Water.
Water who?
Water you answering the door for?

Knock, knock.
Who's there?
Max.
Max who?
Max no difference, can you let me in anyway?

Knock, knock.
Who's there?
Gary.
Gary who?
Gary on smiling!

Knock, knock.
Who's there?
Abby.
Abby who?
Abby birthday to you!

Knock, knock.!
Who's there?
Armageddon.
Armageddon who?
Armageddon out of here!

Knock, knock. .
Who's there?
Irish.
Irish who?
Irish you a Merry Christmas!

Knock, knock.
Who's there?
Lisa.
Lisa who?
Lisa you can do is let me in!

Knock, knock.
Who's there?
Candace.
Candace who?
Candace be the last Knock, knock. joke?

Doctor, Doctor Jokes

Some Stupid Ones

Doctor, Doctor! I feel like a pack of cards.
I'll deal with you later!

Doctor, Doctor! I feel like a spoon.
Then sit still and don't stir!

Doctor, Doctor! Whenever I talk, people ignore me.
Next Please!

Doctor, Doctor! I'm allergic to the high jump.
You'll soon get over it!

Doctor, Doctor! My friend thinks he's a parachute.
Tell him to drop in and see me!

Doctor, Doctor! I have a splitting headache.
I'll need to axe you a few questions!

Doctor, Doctor! I just swallowed a bone.
Are you choking?
No, I really did!

Doctor, Doctor! I'm getting shorter and shorter.
You must be a little patient!

Doctor, Doctor! I'm addicted to brake fluid.
I'm sure you can stop anytime!

Doctor, Doctor! I think I need glasses.
You certainly do - this is a newsagents!

Some General Ones

Doctor, Doctor! I keep comparing things to something else.
Don't worry, it's only analogy.

Doctor, Doctor! I think I'm a bridge.
What's come over you?
So far three cars, a motorbike and a lorry!

Doctor, Doctor! I keep snoring so loudly I wake myself up.
Sleep in another room then!

Doctor, Doctor! I've got terrible wind. Is there anything you can give me?
Yes - have my kite!

Doctor, Doctor! My brother thinks he's a lift.
Why didn't he come in?
He doesn't stop at this floor!

Doctor, Doctor! I'm out of breath.
You must have flu.
No, I definitely walked here!

Doctor, Doctor! I keep losing my memory.
When did this happen?
When did what happen?

Doctor, Doctor! All I can see is blue and yellow spots.
Have you seen a shrink?
No, just the spots!

Doctor, Doctor! My wife thinks she's a traffic warden.
Tell her I'll meter later!

Doctor, Doctor! I keep seeing double.
Sit down on the couch please.
Which one?

Some Classic Ones

Doctor, Doctor! I feel like I'm a pair of curtains.
Pull yourself together man!

Doctor, Doctor! I think I'm a garbage can.
Don't talk rubbish!

Doctor, Doctor! I've only got 59 seconds to live.
Wait a minute, please!

Doctor, Doctor! It hurts wherever I touch myself.
That's because you have a broken finger!

Doctor, Doctor! I think I'm two different people.
One at a time please!

Doctor, Doctor! This is the second time I've broken my leg in the same place.
Then I wouldn't go back there again!

Doctor, Doctor! I think I'm a vampire.
Necks, please!

Doctor, Doctor! I've got acute appendicitis.
You've got a cute face too!

Doctor, Doctor! I think I'm a Shakespearian actor.
It's just a stage you're going through!

Doctor, Doctor! I think I'm a cricket bat.
How's that?

Some Great Advice

Doctor, Doctor! I've just swallowed my pen.
Use a pencil!

Doctor, Doctor! Whenever I drink a cup of coffee, I get a stabbing pain in my eye.
Take the spoon out!

Doctor, Doctor! Can I get a second opinion?
Of course, come back tomorrow.

Doctor, Doctor! Please help me out.
Certainly. Which way did you come in?

Doctor, Doctor! I feel like I'm boiling.
Simmer down, please!

Doctor, Doctor! I think I'm a yo-yo.
Don't string me along!

Doctor, Doctor! I think I'm turning invisible.
Yes, I can see you're not all there!

Doctor, Doctor! I'm totally invisible.
I'm afraid I can't see you now!

Doctor, Doctor! I think I have amnesia.
I'd just go home and forget about it!

Doctor, Doctor! I think I'm Tom Jones.
It's not unusual!

Some Animal Ones

Doctor, Doctor! I think I'm a moth.
Why come and see me?
Well, there was a light on and I couldn't help it...

Doctor, Doctor! I think I'm a spider.
That's just a web of lies!

Doctor, Doctor! I feel shy because I think I'm a snail.
Well we'll soon get you out of your shell!

Doctor, Doctor! I think I'm a caterpillar.
I'm sure that one day you'll change!

Doctor, Doctor! I smell of fish.
Oh you poor sole!

Doctor, Doctor! I keep seeing a spinning insect.
Don't worry, it's just a bug that's going around.

Doctor, Doctor! I think I'm a dog.
Sit!

Doctor, Doctor! I think I'm an electric eel.
That's shocking!

Doctor, Doctor! I think I'm a pony.
No, you're just a little hoarse!

Doctor, Doctor! I think I'm a goat.
How long have you been like this?
Since I was a kid!

Some With Medicine

Doctor, Doctor! I think I'm a bell.
Take these twice a day and if it doesn't help, give me a ring!

Doctor, Doctor! Do you have anything for a bad headache?
Hit yourself with this hammer - that should do the trick!

Doctor, Doctor! Can you cure my measles?
I'm sorry, I never make rash promises.

Doctor, Doctor! I keep stealing things.
Have you taken anything for it?

Doctor, Doctor! I think I'm a needle.
I can see your point!

Doctor, Doctor! I think I'm a racehorse.
Take one of these every four laps!

Doctor, Doctor! I think I'm Mozart.
I'll be with you in a minuet!

Doctor, Doctor! I think I'm Moses.
I have some tablets for you!

Doctor, Doctor! I think I'm an elevator.
You must be going down with something!

Doctor, Doctor! I think I'm a dollar bill.
Take these pills and see if there's any change in the morning!

Some More General Ones

Doctor, Doctor! I'm worried about my insomnia.
I wouldn't lose any sleep over it!

Doctor, Doctor! I think I'm a small bucket.
Yes, you are a little pail!

Doctor, Doctor! I can't stop playing Scrabble.
My word!

Doctor, Doctor! I can't finish my crosswords. What is wrong with me?
I haven't got a clue!

Doctor, Doctor! I think I'm a camera.
I'll be with you in a flash!

Doctor, Doctor! I keep giving away money.
I'll need to take a few notes!

Doctor, Doctor! I think I'm window and it hurts.
Show me where the pane is!

Doctor, Doctor! I think I'm an accountant.
You've obviously ledger self go!

Doctor, Doctor! I think I'm a race car.
You're probably going round the bend!

Doctor, Doctor! I think I'm a tennis racket.
You're probably highly strung!

Some More With Animals

Doctor, Doctor! I think I'm a beaver.
Well it was nice gnawing you!

Doctor, Doctor! I think I'm an owl.
Don't be such a twit!

Doctor, Doctor! I think I'm a duck.
I'm not a quack, you know!

Doctor, Doctor! I keep getting bitten by a squirrel.
You must be nuts!

Doctor, Doctor! I think I'm a cow.
Pull the udder one!

Doctor, Doctor! I think I'm a bee.
You again? Buzz off!

Doctor, Doctor! I think I'm a snake.
I hope you're not rattled!

Doctor, Doctor! I think I'm a sheep.
That sounds baaaaaaaad!

Doctor, Doctor! I think I'm an elephant!
Try these trunkquilizers!

Doctor, Doctor! I keeping thinking I'm in Watership Down.
Stop rabbiting on!

Some With Food

Doctor, Doctor! I feel like an apple.
I'm sure we can get to the core of this!

Doctor, Doctor! I feel like cheese biscuits.
You're crackers!

Doctor, Doctor! I think I'm a carrot.
Don't get yourself in a stew!

Doctor, Doctor! I can't stop eating Chicken Tikka.
Don't try to curry favour like that!

Doctor, Doctor! I think I'm a raspberry.
Well you're in a jam!

Doctor, Doctor! I've just eaten twenty pancakes.
How waffle!

Doctor, Doctor! There's a strawberry in my ear.
I think I've got some cream for that!

Doctor, Doctor! I have sponge, cream and jelly in my ear.
You must be a trifle deaf!

Doctor, Doctor! I've just eaten a quilt!
I can see you're down in the mouth!

Doctor, Doctor! I'm allergic to liquorice.
Well, it takes allsorts!

Some of the Best Ones

Doctor, Doctor! I can't stop lying.
I find that very hard to believe!

Doctor, Doctor! I'm allergic to perfume.
I'll have you scent to a specialist!

Doctor, Doctor! I'm suffering from Déjà vu.
Didn't I see you yesterday?

Doctor, Doctor! I've swallowed a roll of film.
Let's hope nothing develops!

Doctor, Doctor! I feel like a couple of wig-wams.
I think you're too tense!

Doctor, Doctor! Sorry I'm late, I broke my ankle.
That's a lame excuse!

Doctor, Doctor! I think I'm a drill.
That must be boring!

Doctor, Doctor! I think I'm a comedian.
You must be joking!

Doctor, Doctor! I keep dropping the ball.
I wouldn't worry, it's not catching!

Doctor, Doctor! My feet smell and my nose is running.
I think you were born upside down!

Lightbulb Jokes

General Jokes - Part 1

How many magicians does it take to change a lightbulb?
That depends on what you want it changed into!

How many kids with ADD does it take to change a lightbulb?
Hey! You wanna go ride bikes?

How many Vulcans does it take to change a lightbulb?
One. Any more would be illogical!

How many Nitpicks does it take to change a lightbulb?
None. They just let someone else change it then point out all the mistakes the bulb-changer made!

How many Windows Vista installations does it take to change a lightbulb?
DRIVER_IRQL_NOT_LESS_OR_EQUAL

How many Greenpeace members does it take to change a lightbulb?
Two. One to put in the new one and one to recycle the old one.

How many misers does it take to change a lightbulb?
None, it's cheaper to sit in the dark!

How many Navy SEALS does it take to change a
lightbulb?
*Four. One to change it and three to shout GO! GO!
GO!*

How many pessimists does it take to change a
lightbulb?
*None. It's a waste of time because the new bulb
probably won't work either.*

How many optimists does it take to change a
lightbulb?
*None, they're convinced that the power will come
back on soon.*

Jobs - Part 1

How many accountants does it take to change a
lightbulb?
What sort of answer did you have in mind?

How many censors does it take to change a
lightbulb?
*Three. One to **** the **** whilst the other two ****
because ***!*

How many anglers does it take to change a
lightbulb?
*Five. One to actually change it whilst the other four
tell you how big the one they nearly changed was!*

How many road repairers does it take to change a lightbulb?
Ten. One to screw the new one in whilst the other nine lean around on their shovels.

How many nuclear engineers does it take to change a lightbulb?
Eight. One to install the new bulb, and seven to figure what to do with the old one for the next 10,000 years!

How many safety inspectors does it take to change a lightbulb?
Three. One to change it and two to hold the ladder.

How many cover blurb writers does it take to change a lightbulb?
A vast and teeming horde, stretching from sea to shining sea...

How many auto mechanics does it take to change a lightbulb?
Only one, but he'll have to replace the whole socket and that's expensive...

How many carpenters does it take to change a lightbulb?
No chance mate, that's the electrician's job!

How many Psychiatrists does it take to change a lightbulb?
Only one, but the bulb has got to really want to change.

General Jokes - Part 2

How many autocorrected text messages does it take to change a lightbulb?
Foux! There to eat lemons, axe gravy soup.

How many trainspotters does it take to change a lightbulb?
Two. One to change it and one to write down its serial number.

How many Emo kids does it take to change a lightbulb?
None. They prefer everything black anyway.

How many Beverly Hills residents does it take to change a lightbulb?
None, they have someone to come in and do that.

How many Chinese does it take to change a lightbulb?
Hundreds - Confucius say many hands make light work!

How many Vietnam veterans does it take to change a lightbulb?
You don't Know! You weren't there, man!

How many mutants does it take to change a lightbulb?
Two thirds!

How many nihilists does it take to change a lightbulb?
It doesn't matter, we're all gonna die anyway.

How many teenage girls does it take to change a lightbulb?
Just one, but she'll be on the phone for five hours telling all her friends about it.

How many up-tight Victorian gentlemen does it take to change a lightbulb?
Ahem. We do not discuss this with ladies and children present.

Politics, Religion and Philosophy

How many libertarians does it take to change a lightbulb?
None, because somebody might come into the room who likes to sit in the dark.

How many social scientists does it take to change a lightbulb?
None. They do not change light bulbs - they search for the root cause as to why the last one went out.

How many Trotskyists does it take to change a lightbulb?
It's no use trying to change it, it's got to be SMASHED!

How many Marxists does it take to change a lightbulb?
None: The light bulb contains the seeds of its own revolution.

How many Zen masters does it take to change a lightbulb?
None. Zen masters carry their own light.

How many Christians does it take to change a lightbulb?
Three, but they're really all the same being.

How many Taoists does it take to change a lightbulb?
None. You cannot change a lightbulb. It is what it is.

How many evolutionists does it take to change a lightbulb?
They won't actually try to change the bulb. They'll simply stop using the room that has the burned out bulb, and start using only rooms with functioning bulbs. Over the course of millions of years...

How many TV evangelists does it take to change a lightbulb?
One. But for the message of hope to continue to go forth, send in your donation today.

How many existentialists does it take to change a lightbulb?
Two; one to screw it in, and one to observe how the bulb itself represents a single incandescent beacon of subjective reality in a netherworld of endless absurdity reaching out toward a maudlin cosmos of nothingness.

General Jokes - Part 3

How many Einsteins does it take to change a lightbulb?
That depends on the speed of the changer, and the mass of the bulb. It's all relative!

How many dull people does it take to change a lightbulb?
One.

How many Orthodox Rabbis does it take to change a lightbulb?
Change?

How many egotists does it take to change a lightbulb?
One. They put the bulb in and lets the world revolve around them!

How many Spanish men does it take to change a lightbulb?
Just Juan.

How many Real Men does it take to change a lightbulb?
None. 'Real Men' aren't afraid of the dark.

How many Freudians does it take to change a lightbulb?
Three. One to change the bulb, and two more to argue what the light bulb represents.

How many consultants does it take to change a lightbulb?
I'll have an estimate for you a week from Monday.

How many Mafia hitmen does it take to change a lightbulb?
Three. One to screw it in, one to watch, and one to shoot the witness.

How many Pygmies does it take to screw in a light bulb?
At least three!

Jobs - Part 2

How many secret agents does it take to change a lightbulb?
Two: One to screw it in and the other to check it for bugging devices.

How many economists does it take to change a lightbulb?
None. If the light bulb really needed changing, market forces would have already caused it to happen.

How many lawyers does it take to change a lightbulb?
How many can you afford?

Again, how many lawyers does it take to change a lightbulb?
Two. One to change it and the other to keep interrupting by standing up and shouting "Objection!"

How many software technicians does it take to change in a lightbulb?
None. That's a hardware problem.

How many folk singers does it take to change a lightbulb?
Two. One to change it, the other to write a song about how good the old one was.

How many fashion designers does it take to change a lightbulb?
Ten. One to change it and the other nine to tell him how Fabulous it is.

How many drummers does it take to change a lightbulb?
One, two, and a-one two three four...

How many actors does it take to change a lightbulb?
Only one. They don't like to share the spotlight.

How many telemarketers does it take to change a lightbulb?
One. But he has to do it while you're having dinner.

General Jokes - Part 4

How many amoebae does it take to change a lightbulb?
One. No, two. No, four. No, eight...

How many monkeys does it take to change a lightbulb?
Two. One to do it and one to scratch his bum.

How many cops does it take to change a lightbulb?
None, it turns itself in.

How many antelopes does it take to change a
lightbulb?
*None. They are hardy animals that migrate between
tundra and wide open plains and therefore have no
need for an artificial light source.*

How many sheep does it take to change a lightbulb?
*Twenty-one. One to change it and twenty to follow
him round while he looks for a new one.*

How many seabirds does it take to change a
lightbulb?
About four or five terns ought to do the trick.

How many grocery store cashiers does it take to
change a lightbulb?
*Are you kidding? They won't even change a five
dollar bill!*

How many Bob Dylan fans does it take to change
a lightbulb?
The answer, my friend, is blowin' in the wind.

How many Yale students does it take to change a
lightbulb?
We'll never know, they took an oath not to reveal it.

How many public opinion researchers does it take
to change a lightbulb?
With what degree of certainty do you need to know?

Jobs - Part 3

How many bitter actors does it take to change a lightbulb?
A hundred. One to change the bulb and ninety-nine to say "I could have done that."

How many dentists does it take to change a lightbulb?
Just one, but the next appointment is in two months' time.

How many doctors does it take to change a lightbulb?
None, they'll have to refer you to a specialist.

How many civil servants does it take to change a lightbulb?
Thirty. One to change the bulb, and twenty-nine to do the paperwork.

How many Massage Therapists does it take to change a lightbulb?
One, but they have to have candles and soft music to do it.

How many aerobics instructors does it take to change a lightbulb?
Five. Four to do it in perfect synchrony and one to stand there saying "To the left, and to the left, and to the right, and to the right, and take it out, and put it down, and pick it up, and put it in..."

How many waiters does it take to change a lightbulb?
None, even a burned out bulb can't catch a waiter's eye.

How many talk show hosts does it take to change a lightbulb?
Three, one to screw in the new bulb, one to ask the old one how it feels to be replaced, and one to take questions from the audience.

How many jugglers does it take to change a lightbulb?
One, but it takes at least three light bulbs.

How many archaeologists does it take to change a lightbulb?
Why change it? The broken bulb is a national treasure demonstrating our rich history and culture.

General Jokes - Part 5

How many procrastinators does it take to change a lightbulb?
One - but he has to wait until the light is better.

How many missionaries does it take to change a lightbulb?
One, and thirty natives to see the light.

How many Dario Argento fans does it take to
change a lightbulb?
*Two. One to change it and one to film the demise
of the old one in explicit gory detail, using obscure
camera angles.*

How many mothers-in-law does it take to change a
lightbulb?
*A hundred. One to change it and the other ninety-
nine to say, "I told you so!"*

How many senior citizens does it take to change a
lightbulb?
*One, but she pays a telemarketer $1000 for the
new bulb.*

How many dyslexics does it take to bulb a like
change?
Eno.

How many poltergeists does it take to change a
lightbulb?
*Three. One to unscrew the old bulb and drop it on
the floor, one to put the new bulb in, and one to move
a few more things about just for good measure.*

How many Amish does it take to change a
lightbulb?
Change a what?

How many knock-knock jokes does it take to
change a lightbulb?
Who's there?

How many Les Miserables characters does it take
to change a lightbulb?
Just one, because she's On Her Own.

The Best Ones

How many thought police does it take to change a
lightbulb?
*None. There was never a lightbulb there in the first
place, OK?*

How many cold War Russians does it take to
change a lightbulb?
I can't tell you, that's still classified information!

How many Borg does it take to change a lightbulb?
One, but the whole collective would be aware of it.

How many mystery writers does it take to change
a lightbulb?
*Two: One to screw it almost all the way in and the
other to give it a surprising twist at the end!*

How many voyeurs does it take to change a
lightbulb?
*Only one, but they'd much rather watch someone
else do it!*

How many disco dancers does it take to change a lightbulb?
Two. One to boogie up the ladder and one to say "Get dowwwwwn!"

How many people with OCD does it take to change a lightbulb?
Just the one, but they keep changing it back and forth between the new and old bulbs.

How many customer support technicians does it take to change a lightbulb?
We have received your query concerning your technical lighting issue and have assigned you request number 45884AXT-67. Please use this reference for any future contact regarding the light bulb issue.

One!
How many psychics does it take to change a lightbulb?

How many surrealists does it take to change a lightbulb?
Flags. One to gargle the giraffe and bacon to bacon my gaffer tape at Tuesday concierge.

Spooky
Jokes

General Jokes - Part 1

What happened when a ghost asked for a brandy at his local pub?
The landlord said "Sorry, we don't serve spirits."

What happens to a ghost when he gets lost in the fog?
He is mist!

Why did the vampire give his girlfriend a blood test?
To see if she was his type!

What do you get when you cross a vampire and a snowman?
Frostbite!

What do you call someone who puts poison in a person's corn flakes?
A cereal killer!

Why is a cemetery a great place to write a story?
Because there are so many plots there!

What's the best way to talk to a monster?
From a long way away!

Where do baby ghosts go during the day?
Dayscare centers!

What would you call the ghost of a door-to-door salesman?
A dead ringer!

What room can't a ghost go in?
The Living Room!

Ghosts

Which trees do ghosts like best?
Ceme-trees!

Who writes ghostly jokes?
Crypt writers!

What kind of street does a ghost like best?
A dead end!

What do you call a ghost's mother and father?
Transparents!

What do young ghosts write their homework in?
Exorcise books!

Why are ghosts bad at telling lies?
Because you can see right through them!

Where do ghosts go if they want to swim?
The Dead Sea!

What did the ghost teacher say to her class?
Watch the board and I'll go through it again!

What kind of ghosts haunt operating theatres?
Surgical spirits!

This woman wanted to marry a ghost. I don't know what possessed her!

Witches

Why do witches only ride their brooms after dark?
That's the time to go to sweep!

What is evil, ugly and keep the neighbours awake?
A witch with a drum kit!

What goes cackle, cackle, bonk?
A witch laughing her head off!

What happens if you see twin witches?
You won't be able to tell which witch is which!

Why won't a witch wear a flat cap?
Because there is no point in it!

What kind of tests do they give in witch school?
Hex-aminations!

What happened to the witch who lost her temper
when riding her broom?
She flew off the handle!

What do you call a witch with one leg?
Eileen!

Have you heard about the good weather witch?
She's forecasting sunny spells!

Why is a witch like a candle?
They are both wicked!

General Jokes - Part 2

Do monsters like to eat popcorn with their fingers?
No, they prefer to eat fingers separately!

Why did Dracula go to the library?
He wanted a good book to sink his teeth into!

How do you work a mummy's doorbell?
Just Toot and come in!

What do witches put on their hair?
Scare spray!

When do vampires like horse racing?
When it's neck and neck!

Why did the skeleton go scuba diving?
Because he wanted to get some muscles!

What does a panda ghost eat?
Bam-BOO!

Why are graveyards so noisy?
Because of all the coffin!

Why do ghosts like to ride in elevators?
It raises their spirits!

Why is there always a fence around a cemetery?
Because people are just dying to get in!

Vampires

Where does Dracula keep his valuables?
In a blood bank!

Why are vampires so easy to fool?
Because they're suckers!

What would you get if you crossed a vampire and
a teacher?
Lots of blood tests!

What do vampires enjoy most about baseball?
The bats!

What is a vampires favorite holiday?
Fangsgiving!

What is a vampire's favorite circus act?
Well, he always goes for the juggler!

Why doesn't Dracula have any friends?
Because he's a pain in the neck!

Why are all male vampires related to each other?
They are all blood brothers!

How does a girl vampire flirt?
She bats her eyelashes!

How do you learn more about Dracula?
You join his fang club!

Skeletons

Why didn't the skeleton go to the party?
He had no body to go with!

What do you call a skeleton who won't get up in the mornings?
Lazy bones!

Why are skeletons so calm?
Nothing gets under their skin!

Why couldn't the skeleton sing in public?
He just didn't have the guts!

Who was the most famous French skeleton?
Napoleon bone-apart !

Who was the most famous skeleton detective?
Sherlock Bones!

What is a Skeleton's favorite song?
Bad to the Bone

Why don't skeletons play music in church?
They have no organs!

What does a skeleton order at a restaurant?
Spare ribs!

What do skeletons say before they eat?
Bone Appetite!

Mummies

How do mummies begin their letters?
"Tomb it may concern"!

Why don't mummies take vacations?
They're afraid they'll relax and unwind!

What kind of girl does a mummy take on a date?
Any old girl he can dig up!

What is a Mummy's favorite type of music?
Wrap!

Why was the mummy so tense?
Because he was all wound up!

How do mummies hide?
They wear masking tape!

Why do mummies make excellent spies?
They're good at keeping things under wraps!

Why were ancient Egyptian children confused?
Because their daddies were mummies!

What did the mummy say to the detective?
Let's wrap this case up!

Why don't mummies have hobbies?
Because they're too wrapped up in their work!

General Jokes - Part 3

When do ghosts usually appear?
Just before someone screams!

Which building does Dracula visit in New York?
The Vampire State Building!

What's a monster's favorite play?
Romeo and Ghouliet!

What happened to the guy who didn't pay his exorcist?
He was repossessed!

Why does Dracula consider himself a good artist?
Because he likes to draw blood!

What's the ratio of a pumpkin's circumference to its diameter?
Pumpkin Pi!

What happens when a ghost haunts a theater?
The actors all get stage fright!

Why did the monster eat a fluorescent bulb?
Because he was in need of a light snack!

What did the skeleton order with his drink?
A mop!

What is the most important subject a witch learns in school?
Spelling!

Animals

When is it really unlucky to see a black cat?
When you're a mouse!

What do you call a haunted chicken?
A poultry-geist !

What kind of pets do ghosts have?
Scaredy Cats!

What do you call two spiders that just got married?
Newlywebs!

Why don't bats live alone?
They like to hang out with their friends!

What do you call dead cows that come back to life?
Zombeef!

What is Dracula's favorite kind of dog?
A blood hound!

What did the werewolf eat after he'd had his teeth cleaned?
The dentist!

What's big and green and goes "Oink, Oink?"
Frankenswine!

What did the duck say after he heard a scary joke?
Nothing, he just quacked up!

The Best Jokes

Why didn't the skeleton want to go to school?
His heart wasn't in it!

What is a vampire's favorite fruit?
A nectarine!

Why is there a gate around cemeteries?
Because people are dying to get in!

Why didn't the zombie go to school?
He felt rotten!

Who won the zombie war?
Nobody, it was dead even!

What song do vampires hate?
"You are my sunshine"!

I have 28 legs, 7 arms and 3 heads, what am I?
A liar!

Why are so few ghosts arrested?
It's hard to pin anything on them!

Why do demons and ghouls hang out together?
Because demons are a ghoul's best friend!

Why wasn't there any food left after the monster party?
Because everyone was a goblin!

Animal Jokes

Insects

Why do bees hum?
Because they don't know the words!

What do you call a fly without wings?
A walk!

What did one flea say to the other flea?
Shall we walk or take the dog!

What is the difference between a flea and a wolf ?
One prowls on the hairy, the other howls on the prairie!

Why did the fly never land on the computer?
He was afraid of the world wide web!

Who comes to a picnic but is never invited?
Ants!

Why did the fly fly?
Because the spider spied her!

How do fleas travel from place to place?
By itch-hiking!

What do you call a brainy insect?
A spelling bee!

What is on the ground and also a hundred feet in the air?
A centipede on its back!

At the Seaside

Why was the crab arrested?
Because he kept pinching things!

Who has eight guns and terrorises the ocean?
Billy the Squid!

Why is a fish easy to weigh?
Because it has its own scales!

Why did the lobster blush?
Because the sea weed!

Where do shellfish go to borrow money?
To the prawn broker!

What did the boy octopus say to the girl octopus?
I wanna hold your hand, hand, hand, hand, hand, hand, hand, hand!

How do oysters call their friends?
On their shell phones!

Why are dolphins smarter than humans?
Because they can train a man to stand at the side of a pool and feed them fish!

What did the sardine call the submarine?
A can of people!

What do you call a fish with no eyes?
A fsh!

Birds

Why do birds fly south for the winter?
Because it's too far to walk!

Where does a blackbird go for a drink?
To a crow bar!

Why do seagulls live near the sea?
Because if they lived near the bay, they would be called bagels!

What does a duck have with its cheese?
Quackers!

What do you get when you cross a parrot with a pig?
A bird who hogs the conversation!

Which side of a chicken has the most feathers?
The outside!

Who tells the best chicken jokes?
Comedi-hens!

When is the best time to buy budgies?
When they're going cheap!

What do you get when you cross a parrot with a centipede?
A walkie talkie!

How do you turn a duck into a soul singer?
Put it in an oven and wait until its Bill Withers!

Trunktastic

What goes up slowly and comes down quickly?
An elephant in an elevator!

What do you get when you cross an elephant with
a kangaroo?
Holes all over Australia!

What do you get if you cross an elephant with a
whale?
A submarine with a built-in snorkel!

What do you get if you cross a fish with an
elephant?
Swimming trunks!

Why are elephants wrinkled?
Have you ever tried to iron one?

What do you give an elephant that's going to be
sick?
Plenty of space!

Why do elephants never forget?
Because nobody ever tells them anything!

What time is it when an elephant sits on your fence?
Time to get a new fence!

What is an elephant's favourite sport?
Squash!

How do you get four elephants into a Mini?
Two in the front, two in the back!

Cats and Dogs

What happened to the cat that swallowed a ball of wool?
She had mittens!

What has four legs and an arm?
A happy pit bull!

What happens when a cat eats a lemon?
It becomes a sour puss!

Why does everyone love cats?
Because they're purr-fect!

When is it bad luck to see a black cat?
When you're a mouse!

What does a kitten become after it's three days old?
Four days old!

What could happen if it rained cats and dogs?
You might step in a poodle!

What kind of dog tells the time?
A watch dog!

What did the dog say when he sat on sandpaper?
Ruff!

When does a dog go "moo"?
When it is learning a new language!

Unusual Animals

How do porcupines kiss each other?
Very carefully!

What do penguins sing at a birthday party?
Freeze a Jolly Good Fellow!

Why is it hard to play cards in the jungle?
There are too many cheetahs!

What's small and cuddly and bright purple?
A koala holding his breath!

What do call a bear with no ears?
B!

What's the difference between an injured lion and a wet day?
One pours with rain, the other roars with pain!

Which animal is out of bounds?
A tired kangaroo!

What do you call a camel with no humps?
Humphrey!

How many skunks does it take to stink up a house?
A phew!

What is a crocodile's favourite game?
Snap!

Dinosaurs

Why did the dinosaur cross the road?
Because chickens hadn't been invented back then!

What was the scariest dinosaur?
The Terror-dactyl!

Which dinosaurs were the best policemen?
Tricera-cops!

What has a spiked tail, plates on its back, and sixteen wheels?
A Stegosaurus on roller skates!

How many dinosaurs can you fit in an empty box?
Just one... after that, the box isn't empty anymore!

Which type of dinosaur could jump higher than a house?
Any - a house can't jump!

What is in the middle of dinosaurs?
The letter "s"!

What do you get when dinosaurs crash their cars?
Tyrannosaurus wrecks!

What do you call a dinosaur with no eyes?
Do-ya-think-he-saw-us!

What's as big as a dinosaur but weighs nothing?
A dinosaur's shadow!

On the Farm

Where do cows go with their friends?
The moooovies!

Why do cows wear bells?
Their horns don't work!

What do you give a sick pig?
Oink-ment!

Why did the police arrest the turkey?
They suspected it of fowl play!

What kind of animal goes OOM?
A cow walking backwards!

What happened to the lost cattle?
Nobody's herd!

Why did the cow cross the road?
To get to the udder side!

What do you get if you cross a chicken with a cow?
Roost beef!

What is a sheep's favourite game?
Baa-dminton!

What's the most musical part of a chicken?
The drumstick!

Wet and Slimy

What happens when a frog's car breaks down?
He gets toad away!

What did one frog say to the other?
Time's fun when you're having flies!

What is the difference between school dinners and a pile of slugs?
School dinners come on a plate!

What do slugs do at the beach?
Nothing!

What is the strongest animal?
A snail. He carries his house on his back!

What is a snake's favorite subject?
Hiss-tory!

What do you call a snake who works for the government?
A civil serpent!

How do snails get their shells so shiny?
They use snail varnish!

What kind of snake is good at numbers?
An adder!

What did the grape say when the Komodo Dragon stood on it?
Nothing, it just let out a little wine!

Horseplay

What type of horses only go out in the dark?
Nightmares!

What kind of loaf does a horse eat?
Thoroughbred!

How do you say hungry horse in 4 letters?
MTGG!

What do you call a horse wearing venetian blinds?
A zebra!

How did the rabbit propose to his girlfriend?
With a twenty-four carrot ring!

Did you hear about the horse with the negative altitude?
She always said Neigh!

What do you give a sick horse?
Cough stirrup!

What is the difference between a horse and a duck?
One goes quick and the other goes quack!

Why did the farmer ride his horse to town?
It was too heavy to carry!

What do you ask a sad horse?
"Why the long face?"

Funny Book Titles

General Titles – Part 1

Robots by Anne Droid

Songs from 'South Pacific' by Sam and Janet Evening

Karate and Judo by Marsha Larts

Pain in My Body by Otis Leghurts

She Was Naked by Oliver Klozoff

Fixing Computer Programs by Dee Bugger

How to Write a Will by Benny Fishery

Predicting the Future by Claire Voyant

It Won't Work! by Mel Function

It's All In Your Head by Madge Ination

Out and About

The Tragedy Near the Cliff by Ilene Dover

Falling Trees by Tim Burr

Danger! by Luke Out

Never Gonna Happen by Jason Rainbows

Almost Missed the Bus by Justin Time

Highway Travel by Dusty Rhodes

Ambulance Driving by Adam Muhway

The Hitchhiker by Juan Nalift

French Overpopulation by Francis Crowded

World Leaders by Polly Tickell

At School

I Love Mathematics by Adam Up

Body Parts by Anne Atomy

Circle Perimeters by Sir Cumference

The History of the Cold War by Sophie Etunion

Flips and Tumbles by Jim Nastics

How to Succeed in School by Rita Book

Explosives in Chemistry by Stan Wellback

You Did Exceptionally Well by Marco de Stinction

Every Word Ever by Dick Shunnery

A History of Communist Leaders by Dick Tater

General Titles - Part 2

Jewish Holidays by Hannah Kerr

Chest Pain by I. Coffalot

Money Management by Owen Cash

Woodworm Trouble by Nora Bedpost

Nuclear Explosives by Adam Baum

Songs for Children by Barbara Blacksheep

To Be Honest by Frank Lee

Keep On Trying by Percy Veer

A New Dawn Coming by Tamara Morning

I'm Highly Embarrassed by Rosie Cheeks

In Your Home

Carpet Fitting by Walter Wall

Sitting Down at the Barbeque by Patty O'Furniture

Interior Decorating by Curt Enrod

Old Furniture by Anne Teak

Bubbles in the Bathtub by Ivor Windybottom

Artificial Fabrics by Polly Ester

Japanese Clothing by Kim Ono

He Cuts the Grass by Moses Lawn

Repairing Old Clothes by Fred Bear

A Strong Hurricane by Rufus Gone

Crime and Punishment

Theft and Robbery by Andy Tover

Armed Heists by Robin Banks

Breaking the Law by Kermit A. Krime

Crackdown on Violent Crime by Lauren Order

Police Headquarters by Scott Linyard

I Didn't Do It by Ivan Alibi

I Admit That It Was Me by Gil Tea.

Crime Doesn't Pay by Laura Norda

Catching Criminals by Hans Upp

The Policeman and the Criminal by Iris Tew

The Worst Titles

The Runaway Horse by Gay Topen

Telephone Problems by Ron Number

Aching Joints by Arthur Itis

A Load of Old Rubbish by Stefan Nonsense

Will He Win? by Betty Wont

Sunday Service by Neil Downe

Blackpool Beach by Rhoda Donkey

Late Again by Misty Buss

Breakfast in Europe by Roland Butter

Win the Lottery by Jack Pot

General Titles - Part 3

Creaky Door by Rusty Hinges

Cry Wolf by Al Armist

Visiting Haunted Houses by Hugo First

Mosquito Bites by Ivan Itch

A Bestiary of Plant Eaters by Herb Avore

Lizards Taking Over the World by E. Gwanna and Sally Manda

Pain and Sorrow by Anne Guish

A Terrible Journey by Helen Back

Vegetable Gardening by Rosa Cabbages

Cheese Dishes by Della Katessan

Every One A Winner

Dance Dance Dance by Sheik Yabuti

For the Betterment of Society by Ben Everlent

Keep the Animals In by Barb Dwyer

Gardening Equipment by Lon Moore

Come to My Party by Morris Merrier

The Atheist by Noel Noevan

Comedy Today by Stan Dupp

Modern Giants by Hugh Mungus

Dogs are Great by Kay Nein

Leather Preparation by Tanya Hyde

The Best Titles

Irish Flooring by Lynn O'Leum

Artificial Weightlessness by Andy Gravity

Remind Me of Your Name by Hugh R. Ewe

Without Warning by Oliver Sudden

Don't Drink the Potion by Jacqueline Hyde

A Trip To The Dentist by Lord Howard Hurts

Monkeys and Other Primates by Jim Panzee

House Construction by Bill Jerome Holme

Unknown Instructions by Mr. Emmanuel

The Cat's Revenge by Claude Balls

Space Jokes

Astronauts

What is a spaceman's favorite chocolate?
A Mars bar!

Where would an astronaut park his space ship?
A parking meteor!

In what did the astronaut serve drinks?
Sunglasses!

What did the astronaut cook for lunch?
An unidentified frying object!

Why don't astronauts get hungry after being blasted into space?
Because they've just had a big launch!

What does an astronaut do when he gets angry?
He blasts off!

What do you call a loony spaceman?
An astronut.

What is an astronauts favorite computer key?
The space bar!

How do spacemen pass the time on long trips?
They play astro-noughts and crosses!

What do astronauts put on their toast?
Space Jam!

Aliens

What did the alien say to the garden?
Take me to your weeder!

Why don't aliens eat clowns?
Because they taste funny!

What did the alien say when he was out of room?
I'm all spaced out!

What do you call an alien with three eyes?
An aliiien!

What did the alien say to the cat?
Take me to your litter!

What do you call an overweight ET?
An extra cholesterol!

What did the alien say to the gas pump?
Don't you know its rude to stick your finger in your ear when I'm talking to you!

What kind of fur do you get from an Alien?
As fur away as possible!

Where do aliens drink beer?
At the Mars Bar!

What do aliens on the metric system say?
Take me to your liter!

Animals in Space

Why did the cow go to outer space?
To visit the milky way.

How did it get there?
It flew through udder space!

What are the slowest creatures in the galaxy?
Snail-iens!

What does a Klingon frog use for camouflage?
A croaking device!

Why did the cow go in the spaceship?
It wanted to see the mooooooon!

What kind of saddle do you put on a horse in space?
A saddle-lite!

Which creepy-crawly can never go into space?
An earthworm!

What do you call a chicken from outer space?
An egg-straterrestrial!

Why did Mickey Mouse go to outer space?
He was looking for Pluto!

How did the lamb go into outer space?
On a rocket sheep!

Stupid Jokes

What's a light-year?
The same as a regular year, but with less calories!

What did the star say to the black hole?
You suck!

How does a robot shave?
With a laser blade!

Why did Captain Kirk go into the ladies toilet?
To boldly go where no man has been before!

What do planets like to read?
Comet books!

Why did the people not like the restaurant on the moon?
Because there was no atmosphere!

Why is an astronaut like a American Football player?
They both want touchdown!

What do you call an alien starship that drips water?
A crying saucer!

Do robots have brothers?
No, just transistors!

Why did the astronomer hit himself on the head one afternoon?
So he could see the stars during the day as well!

The Solar System

Why did the sun go to school?
To get brighter!

How do you know when the moon has enough to eat?
When it's full!

How do you know that the sun is clean?
It always shines!

How does the solar system hold up its trousers?
With an asteroid belt!

Why didn't the sun go to college?
Because it already had a million degrees!

How do we know Saturn was married more than once?
Because he has a lot of rings!

What kind of music do planets sing?
Neptunes!

What did Mars say to Saturn?
Give me a ring sometime!

Why couldn't the astronaut book a room on the moon?
Because it was full!

Why are the Earth and the Moon good friends?
Because they've been going around together for years!

Star Wars - Part 1

How did Darth Vader know what Luke got for Christmas?
He felt his presents!

What do you call a Mexican Jedi?
Obi-Juan Kenobi!

Why does Princess Leia keep her hair tied up in buns?
So it doesn't hang so low!

Why did Darth Vader cross the road?
To get to the dark side!

What do you get if you mix a fruit with a bounty hunter?
Mango Fett!

What do you call a robot who always takes the longest route?
R2-detour!

Why do doctors make the best Jedi?
Because a Jedi must have patience!

How did Wicket cross the road?
Ewoked!

What do you call a transparent robot?
See-through P O!

How is duck tape like the Force?
It has a Dark Side, a Light side and it binds the galaxy together!

General Jokes

What do planets like to read?
Comet books!

How did the rocket lose its job?
It was fired!

What happens to astronauts who misbehave?
They're grounded!

Which are the most dangerous things in space?
Shooting stars!

What did the boy rocket say to the girl rocket?
Let's go out to launch!

Why did the cow jump over the moon?
Because the farmer had cold hands!

How does one astronaut tell another that he is sorry?
He Apollo-gises.

Why don't astronauts relate well to other people?
They are not always down-to-earth!

What should an astronaut do when he gets dirty?
Take a meteor shower!

What do you call a magician in space?
A flying sorcerer!

Star Wars - Part 2

What side of an Ewok has the most hair?
The outside!

When did Anakin's Jedi masters know he was leaning towards the dark side?
In the Sith Grade!

How many Sith Lords does it take to change a light bulb?
None - they prefer it on the dark side!

Which Star Wars character works at a restaurant?
Darth Waiter!

What do Jedi use to view PDF files?
Adobe Wan Kenobi

Why was Yoda good at gardening?
Because he had green fingers!

Why shouldn't you ask Yoda for money?
Because he's always a little short.

What's the difference between an ATAT and a stormtrooper?
One's an Imperial walker and the other is a walking Imperial!

What is R2-D2 short for?
Because he has small legs!

What do Gungans put Jam in?
Jar Jars!

The Worst Jokes

Why do aliens make crop circles?
Because they are corny.

How many Borg does it take to change a light-bulb?
All of them!

Which astronaut wears the biggest helmet?
The one with the biggest head

What is the centre of gravity?
The letter v!

How many letters are there in the alphabet?
21 - ET left in a UFO

Which is more useful, the Sun or the Moon?
The Moon because the Sun only shines during the day when it's light anyway

Where do dumb aliens go?
Area 52

What do astronauts wear to keep warm?
Apollo-neck sweaters!

How do astronauts eat their ice cream?
In floats

Why is the moon bald?
It has no 'air.

The Best Jokes

How do we know life down under came from outer space?
Because of the Mars-upials and the Austr-aliens!

What's round, purple and orbits the sun?
The Planet of the Grapes!

What did Spock find in Kirk's toilet?
The Captain's Log!

Why didn't the dog star laugh at this joke?
It was too Sirius.

How does the man in the moon cut his hair?
Eclipse it!

How many ears did captain Kirk have?
Three - a left ear, a right ear and a final front-ear!

On what kind of plates do they serve food in space?
Flying saucers!

How do you get a baby astronaut to go to sleep?
Rocket!

How do you organize a space party?
You planet!

Where does Dr Who buy his cooked meat?
At a dalek-atessen!

Food Jokes

General Jokes - Part 1

Why do the French like to eat snails?
Because they don't like fast food!

Why shouldn't you buy exploding alphabetti spaghetti?
If it goes off it could spell disaster!

Why shouldn't you tell an egg a joke?
Because it might crack up!

What is green and sings?
Elvis Parsley!

How do you make a walnut laugh?
Crack it up!

What Italian food do ghosts eat?
Pasta a-fraid-o!

What does an evil hen lay?
Deviled eggs!

What do sea monsters eat for lunch?
Fish and ships!

What did the mayonnaise say when someone opened the refrigerator?
Close the door, I'm dressing!

Where do tough chickens come from?
Hard-boiled eggs!

Cheese

What's the best cheese to hide a horse?
Mascarpone!

What's orange and doesn't belong to you?
Nacho cheese!

Which genre of music appeals to most cheeses?
R'n'Brie

What does cheese say to itself in the mirror?
Halloumi.

What's a Pirate's favourite cheese?
Chedd-Arrrrrrr!

What cheese do you use to lure a bear down a mountain?
Camembert!

How do you approach an angry welsh cheese?
Caerphilly!

What hotel do mice stay in?
The Stilton

What happened after an explosion at a French cheese factory?
All that was left was de brie.

A child threw a block of mild cheese through my window today.
I ran after him and shouted "Well that's not very mature..."

Fruit & Veg - Part 1

Why shouldn't you tell a secret on a farm?
Because the potatoes have eyes and the corn has ears!

Why didn't the fig go to the prom?
He couldn't get a date!

Why did the banana go to the doctor?
Because it wasn't peeling well!

What are twins' favorite fruit?
Pears!

If a crocodile makes shoes, what does a banana make?
Slippers!

What is square and green?
A lemon in disguise!

How do you make an artichoke?
Strangle it!

What's the fastest vegetable?
A runner bean!

What is small, round and giggles a lot?
A tickled onion!

What's the strongest vegetable?
A muscle sprout!

Snacks and Suchlike

Why did the biscuit cry?
Because his dad been a wafer so long!

Did you hear the joke about the peanut butter?
I'm not telling you. You might spread it!

What do you call candy that was stolen?
Hot chocolate!

What did the baby corn say to the mama corn?
Where's pop?

What did the nut say when it sneezed?
Cashew!

Why was the cucumber mad?
Because it was in a pickle!

Why did the baker stop making doughnuts?
She was bored with the hole business!

What's a pilot's favourite crisp flavour?
Plane!

What's a frog's favourite crisp?
Croaky bacon!

Two peanuts walk into a really rough bar.
Unfortunately, one was a salted!

Waiter, Waiter!

Waiter, waiter! What's this fly doing in my soup?
I think it's the backstroke, sir!

Waiter, waiter! This chicken only has one leg.
Perhaps its been in a fight, sir.
In that case bring me the winner!

Waiter, waiter! There's a twig in my soup.
Hold on sir, I'll get the branch manager!

Waiter, waiter! This egg is bad.
It's not my fault sir, I only laid the table!

Waiter, waiter! I can't eat this terrible food.
It's no good complaining to me - I won't eat it either!

Waiter, Waiter! There's no chicken in the chicken soup.
That's alright, sir. There's no horse in the horseradish either!

Waiter, waiter, This coffee tastes like mud!
I'm not surprised sir, it was ground this morning!

Waiter, Waiter! This fish is very rude.
Yes sir, it doesn't know its plaice.

Waiter, Waiter, do you serve lobster?
Bring him in sir, we're not fussy who we serve here!

Waiter, Waiter there's a crocodile in my soup.
Well sir, you told me to make it snappy!

The Worst Jokes

Jack asked Jimmy "If you have four onions and I ask you for one, how many do you have left?"
Jimmy said "If it's you that asked, four!"

Knock knock... Who's there... Turnip... Turnip who?
Turnip for school on time or you'll be expelled!

Where does the lettuce go to have a few drinks?
The salad bar!

Why did the orange stop running?
It ran out of juice!

What did the lettuce say to the celery?
Quit stalking me!

How does a penguin make pancakes?
With its flippers!

Why couldn't the toadstool fit in the pie?
Because there wasn't mush room!

What's worse than finding a worm in your apple?
Finding half a worm in your apple!

How can you tell if an elephant has been in your refrigerator?
Footprints in the cheesecake!

What is green and goes to a summer camp?
A Brussels scout!

General Jokes - Part 2

What does Doctor Who eat with his pizza?
Dalek bread!

Why did the tomato blush?
Because it saw the salad dressing!

Where do burgers like to dance?
At a meat ball!

What did the hungry computer eat?
Chips, one byte at a time!

What do you give to a sick lemon?
Lemon aid!

What's the worst thing you're likely to find in the school cafeteria?
The food!

What day do potatoes hate the most?
Fry-day!

What is a scarecrow's favorite fruit?
Straw-berries!

What's a penguin's favorite salad?
Iceberg lettuce!

Did you hear about the Italian chef who died?
He pasta way!

Fruit & Veg – Part 2

Why were the apple and the orange all alone?
Because the banana split!

Where do baby gorillas sleep?
Ape-ricots!

What key do you use to open a banana?
A monkey!

Why did the people dance to the vegetable band?
Because it had a good beet!

How did the farmer fix his jeans?
With a cabbage patch!

What vegetable might you find in your basement?
Cellar-y!

What does corn get when you leave it in the barn too long?
Cob-webs!

Which vegetable can't you take on a boat?
Leeks!

What did the salad say to the dressing?
Lettuce be friends!

Why did the man at the orange juice factory lose his job?
He couldn't concentrate!

Desserts and Drinks

What do you call someone with jelly in one ear and custard in the other?
A trifle deaf!

How do you make an apple turnover?
Push it down a hill!

What's the fastest cake in the world?
Scone!

Why did the students eat their homework?
Because the teacher said that it was a piece of cake!

What is an elf's favorite kind of treat?
Shortcake!

In which school do you learn to make ice cream?
Sundae School!

How do astronauts eat their ice creams?
In floats!

What did the grape say when the elephant stood on it?
Nothing. It just let out a little whine!

How do you make a milk shake?
Give it a good scare!

What do you get when you cross a frog and a ice
lolly?
A hopsicle!

The Best Jokes

What did the angry customer at the Italian
restaurant give the chef?
A pizza of his mind!

What can you make from onions and baked beans?
Tear gas!

How do you make a gold soup?
Add twenty-four carrots!

Doctor, doctor, I've got a cucumber in my ear, an
apple up my nose and a parsnip in my armpit.
You need to eat more sensibly!

What's orange and sounds like a parrot?
A carrot!

What vegetables do librarians like?
Quiet peas!

What did a pirate pay for his corn?
A buccaneer!

Why was the mushroom invited to the party?
Because he's a fun-guy!

What is small, red and whispers?
A hoarse radish!

A man was drowned eating his muesli the other day. He was pulled in by a strong currant!

What Do You Call Jokes

General Jokes - Part 1

What do you call a woman in a high wind?
Gail

What do you call a man who can't stand?
Neil

What do you call a man who always lies on the floor?
Matt

What do you call a fish with no eyes?
a fsh

What do you call a man correcting homework?
Mark

What do you call a man drilling holes in pieces of wood?
Boring

What do you call a man at the side of a house?
Ali

What do you call a Hippy's wife?
Mississippi

What do you call a man buried in a bog?
Pete

What do you call a woman on a Scottish Hillside?
Heather

Animals - Part 1

What do you call a woman with a cat on her head?
Kitty

What do you call a blind moose?
No idea

What do you call a blind moose with no legs?
Still no idea

What do you call a fly with no wings?
A walk

What do you call a crazy blackbird?
A raven lunatic

What do you call bears without ears?
B

What do you call a rooster who wakes you up every morning?
An alarm cluck

What do you call a vet with a bad throat?
A hoarse doctor

What do you call a rabbit who raps?
a hip hopper

What do you call a sheep with no legs?
A cloud

Things on a Man's Head

What do you call a man with a spade on his head?
Doug

What do you call a man without a spade on his head?
Douglas

What do you call a man with a car on his head?
Jack

What do you call a man with a toilet on his head?
Lou

What do you call a man with a map on his head?
Miles

What do you call a man with a car number plate on his head?
Reg

What do you call a man with a stamp on his head?
Frank

What do you call a man with a boat on his head?
Bob

What do you call a man with a legal document on his head?
Will

What do you call an American with a rabbit on his head?
Hutch

General Jokes - Part 2

What do you call a woman who plans to take you to court?
Sue

What do you call a man who climbs through your letterbox?
Bill

What do you call a man who climbs through a student's letterbox?
Grant

What do you call a man doing exercises?
Jim

What do you call a pig that does karate?
A pork chop

What do you call a man holding a spear?
Lance

What do you call a man holding loads of spears?
Lancelot

What do you call a man with a wig on his head?
Aaron

What do you call a mushroom who is always smiling?
A fungi

What do you call a fake noodle?
An impasta

Animals - Part 2

What do you call a man with a seagull on his head?
Cliff

What do you call a man who has scratches from his cat all over his face?
Claude

What do you call a woman with a tortoise on her head?
Shelley

What do you call a country gentleman with a rabbit on his head?
Warren

What do you call a one-eyed dinosaur?
Doyouthinkhesaurus

What do you call a cow that's just had a baby?
Decalfinated

What do you call an exploding ape?
A baboom

What do you call a snake who is employed by the government?
A civil serpent

What do you call a man who sits under a cow all day?
Pat

What do you call a camel without a hump?
Humphrey

Things on a Woman's Head

What do you call a woman with two toilets on her head?
Lulu

What do you call a woman with a sprig on Holly on her head?
Carol

What do you call a woman with a radiator on her head?
Anita

What do you call a woman with a tennis racket on her head?
Annette

What do you call a woman with slate on her head?
Ruth

What do you call a woman with a pint of ale on her head?
Beatrix

What do you call a woman with a pint of ale on her head and a handful of clay?
Beatrix Potter

What do you call a woman with a pack of cards on her head?
Trixie

What do you call a woman with a twig on her head?
Hazel

What do you call a woman with a frog on her head?
Lily

What are You Wearing?

What do you call a man in a kilt?
Scott

What do you call a man in a suit made from candy wrappers?
Russell

What do you call a man with a coat on his head?
Mac

What do you call a man with two coats on his head?
Max

What do you call a man with two coats on his head in a cemetery?
Max Bygraves

What do you call a man with a large coat on his head?
Big Mac

What do you call a woman with one trouser-leg missing?
Jean

What do you call a man wearing a very tight suit?
Justin

What do you call a man wearing a wooden hat?
Edward

What do you call a man wearing three wooden hats?
Edward Woodward

The Worst Jokes

What do you call two Mexicans playing basketball together?
Juan 'n' Juan

What do you call a man who is short-sighted?
Piers

What do you call a woman who is levitating?
Rose

What do you call a man in a cathedral window?
Archie

What do you call a man on a roof?
Tyler

What do you call a woman who prays before eating?
Grace

What do you call a woman with her head in a book?
Paige

What do you call a woman with her head in the clouds?
Skye

What do you call a shoe made from a banana?
A slipper

What do you call someone who is scared of Santa?
A Claus-trophobic

General Jokes - Part 3

What do you call a boomerang that doesn't come back?
A stick

What do you call a sleepwalking nun?
A roamin' Catholic

What do you call a cow with two legs?
Lean beef

What do you call a cow with no legs?
Ground beef

What do you call a man who isn't religious?
Godfrey

What do you call a man packed tightly into a hole?
Phil

What do you call a woman sitting on a loaf of bread?
Marge

What do you call a woman with one leg either side
of a river?
Bridget

What do you call a man driving a truck?
Laurie

What do you call a group of cows with a sense of
humour?
A laughing stock

The Best Jokes

What do you call two men in the window?
Kurt 'n' Rod

What do you call a woman with only one leg?
Eileen

What do you call a woman with a sunlamp on her
head?
Tanya

What do you call a woman with a laptop on her
head?
Adele

What do you call a Frenchman wearing beach shoes?
Phillipe Phillope

What do you call a grammatically incorrect lion?
An lion

What do you call a man with a purple mark on his head?
Bruce

What do you call cheese that isn't yours?
Nacho cheese

What do you call a fat psychic?
A four-chin teller

What do you call a Mexican whose Ford was stolen?
Carlos

And Finally...

What do you call a judge with no thumbs?
Justice Fingers

www.ingramcontent.com/pod-product-compliance
Lightning Source LLC
Chambersburg PA
CBHW031256060726

47590CB00003B/934